Bass Guitar Songbook

Christmas Carols and Classics for Bass Guitar

Adrian Gavinson

Adrian Gavinson

MERRY CHRISTMAS

I wish you a merry Christmas and a happy new year full of joy and happiness. May all your dreams and wishes for the new year come true.

From all of us at *A&M* Books

Adrian Gavinson

CONTENTS

Adrian Gavinson

Bass Guitar Songbook:
Christmas Carols and Classics For Bass Guitar

Silent Night

```
G|————————————-—-—————-——————————|
D|————7————9—————7—————————————-—|
A|————0————————————————————————9————|
E|——————————-————————————————————————|


G|————————————-—-—————-——————————|
D|————7————9—————7——————————————-—|
A|————0————————————————————————9————|
E|——————————-————————————————————————|


G|———9———9—————-—6—--7-7————-————|
D|————————————————————————————-7————|
A|—————————————————————————————-————-—|
E|—————————-——————————————————-———|
```

```
G|----0--------.---7----6--.--------.--|
D|----9-.------------------------9----.-|
A|--------------.-----------------------.---|
E|-----------.---.----------------------|


G|---------------.---.--------.----------.--|
D|----7--------9-----7-----------------.--|
A|---5-------------------------9----.---|
E|-----------.------------------------.---|


G|---9-----9--.--.------7--.---6-----|
D|---0-----0-------------------------9.--|
A|-------------------------------.------.-|
E|-----------.--------------------.--|
```

```
G|————————————·——·——————————·——————·———|
D|———7————————9——————7——————————————|
A|—————————————————————————————9———·——|
E|——————————·—·——————————————————————·——|
```

```
G|—————9——————-9——·—12—9——·—·————|
D|————7————————————————————·—|
A|———————————————————————————————·———·—·—|
E|————————·—————————————————·——|
```

```
G|————6——————7·——·—————·—11————|
D|——————————0————————————·—|
A|—————————————————————·———|
E|—————————·———————————————|
```

```
G|-----7---------.---.---------------.----|
D|---------7--------------7--------.-|
A|-------------------9----------------|
E|---------.------------------------|
```

```
G|-----------------.---.-----.------------|
D|----------------------------------.-|
A|--------9---7-----5---------.---|
E|-------.-------------------------|
```

```
G|----------------.--.-------.--7-------|
D|-------------7------------------.-|
A|------------------------------------|
E|-------.----------------.---|
```

```
G|------------------------.-----.----------.---------------|
D|-----7-----9-------7--------------------------.--|
A|-----0--------------------------------------9----|
E|------------.--------------------------------------|


G|------------------.-------.-------------.---------------|
D|-----7-----9-------7-----------------------.--|
A|-----0--------------------------------------9----|
E|------------.---------------------------------------|


G|----9---9-----.--6--.--7-7-----.------|
D|-------------------------------------7-----|
A|----------------------------------.-----.--|
E|-------------.-------------------------.----|
```

```
G|————0————————·———7————6——·—————————·—|
D|————·9·—————————————————————————9—————·|
A|————————————·——————————————————————·———|
E|————————————·———·—————————————————————|
```

```
G|————————————————————·——·————————————————·——|
D|————·7—————————9—————7————————————————·—|
A|———5——————————————————————————9———·———|
E|————————————·—————————————————————·————|
```

```
G|———9—————9——·———·————7——·———6——————|
D|———0—————0————————————————————————9·——|
A|———————————————————————————————·————·—|
E|—————————·——————————————————————·—|
```

```
G|————————————-—--—————————-—————-—-——|
D|————7————————9————————7————————————|
A|——————————————————————————————9——--——|
E|———————————-——————————————————-—-——|
```

```
G|————9————————-9———-—12——9——-.————|
D|————7———————————————————————————-—|
A|—————————————————————————————-——-—|
E|—————————-—————————————————-——|
```

```
G|————6————————7-——-—————--—11—————|
D|————————————0————————————————-—|
A|————————————————————————————-——|
E|————————-——————————————————————|
```

```
G|-----7------------------.------.-------------------.---|
D|------------7-------------------------7---------.-|
A|----------------------9-----------------------|
E|---------------.-------------------------------|
```

```
G|-----------------------.------.------------.-----------|
D|--------------------------------------------.-|
A|----------9----7-----5--------------.---|
E|-------------.--------------------------------|
```

```
G|---------------------.-------.--------------.-7--------|
D|---------------7-----------------------------.-|
A|---------------------------------------------|
E|--------------.-----------------------.----|
```

Joy To The World

```
G|----7------6--·---·-4------·2--------|
D|----0--------------------------·--|
A|----------------------------·-·---|
E|----------·---------------·------|
```

```
G|------------·---·--·----·---------|
D|----5----4---2-------0------·--|
A|--------------------------0----·----|
E|--------------------------------|
```

```
G|----2-----4--·-4--6--6--·--·-7--|
D|----------------------------·--|
A|----------------------------·---|
E|-------·-------------------|
```

```
G|----------------------------------------|
D|----------------------0-----------------|
A|----------------------------------------|
E|----------------------------------------|
```

```
G|----7-----7---6---6---4--2-2-|
D|----------------------------------------|
A|----------------------------------------|
E|----------------------------------------|
```

```
G|----------------------------------------|
D|--------5--------4----------------------|
A|----------------------------------------|
E|----------------------------------------|
```

```
G|--7---7--6---·---4----2---2---|
D|----------------------------·-|
A|-------------------------·----|
E|--------·---------------------|


G|------------·---------·-------|
D|--------5----4--------4----|
A|-----------------------·----|
E|-------·----------------------|


G|-------------·---·----·-------|
D|---4----4--4---4----------·-|
A|-----------------------·----|
E|------·-----------------------|
```

```
G|------------------------------------|
D|------4-----5-----7-----------------|
A|------------------------------------|
E|------------------------------------|
```

```
G|------------------------------------|
D|------5-------4---------2---2---2-|
A|------------------------------------|
E|------------------------------------|
```

```
G|------------------------------------|
D|------2-------4-----5-----------------|
A|------------------------------------|
E|------------------------------------|
```

```
G|-----------4-------2-----------0------|
D|-----4-------2-----------0------|
A|-------------------------------------|
E|-------------------------------------|
```

```
G|----------7------------------------|
D|-------------------------------------|
A|-------------------------------------|
E|-------------------------------------|
```

```
G|----4---2--0-----------------|
D|--------------------4--------|
A|-------------------------------|
E|-------------------------------|
```

```
G|-----6-------.----------------.---------.--|
D|-----------4---2----0-------.--|
A|-------------------------------.----|
E|--------.------------------------------|
```

```
G|---7-------6--.----.-4-------2-------|
D|---0----------------------------------.--|
A|------------------------------.--.----|
E|------------.--------------------.-------|
```

```
G|--------------------.----.-----------.---------|
D|---5---4---2----------0-------.--|
A|---------------------------0------.---|
E|-------------------------------------|
```

```
G|———2————4———·—4——6——6——·———7——|
D|——————————————————————————·—|
A|———————————————————————·——|
E|——————·———————————————————|
```

```
G|————————————·———·———————·————|
D|———————————————0————————————|
A|————————————————————————·——|
E|————————·—————————————————|
```

```
G|————7————7—·——6———6·——4——2-2—|
D|————————————————·————————·—|
A|—————————————————·———————·——|
E|——————·———————·——————————|
```

```
G|———————————-——-——————-—————|
D|——————5————————4——————————-————-—|
A|—————————————————————————————-———|
E|———————————-——————————————————————|
```

```
G|——7————7——6——-——-————4————2———2———|
D|————————————————————————————————-——|
A|——————————————————————————————-———|
E|————————-————————————————————————|
```

```
G|———————————-———-————————-————————|
D|—————————5————4————————4-—————|
A|—————————————————————————————-——|
E|———————-————————————————————————|
```

```
G|——————————————-—-—————-—————————|
D|———4————4——4———4———————————-—|
A|———————————————————————————-———|
E|—————————-————-———————————————|
```

```
G|—————————————-——-—————————-————|
D|——————4————5————7———————————-—|
A|—————————————————————————————-———|
E|——————————-————————————————————|
```

```
G|———————————————-———-——————-————————|
D|————5——————4————————2———2———2—|
A|————————————————————————————————-———|
E|———————————-—————————————————|
```

```
G|——————————————·—·——————————————·————————————|
D|————2——————4————5————————————————————·——|
A|——————————————————————————————————————————·———|
E|—————————·——————————————————————————————|
```

```
G|———————————————————·——·—————————·———————|
D|————4———————2—————————————0————·——|
A|——————————————————————————————————————·———|
E|—————————·——————————————————————————|
```

```
G|—————————7—·———·————————————————|
D|——————————————————————————————·—|
A|——————————————————————————————·——|
E|—————————·——————————————————————|
```

```
G|————4———2——0——·————————·————————|
D|————————————————————————4————————|
A|————————————————————————————·————|
E|————————————·————————————————————|


G|—————6————————·————·————————·———·—|
D|—————————————4———2————0—————————·—|
A|—————————————————————————————·———|
E|————————————·—————————————————————|


G|———7—————6——·———·—4—————-2—————-—|
D|———0————————————————————————————·—|
A|————————————————————————————·——·———|
E|——————————·————————————————·————————|
```

```
G|————————————·—·—————·————————|
D|———5————4———2—————————0—————————·—|
A|———————————————————————0————·———|
E|—————————————————————————————————|
```

```
G|———2————4——·—4——6——6—·————7——|
D|——————————————————————————————·—|
A|———————————————————————————·————|
E|————————·————————————————————————|
```

```
G|——————————————·——·————·——————————|
D|————————————————0————————————————|
A|————————————————————————————·————|
E|———————·—————————————————————————|
```

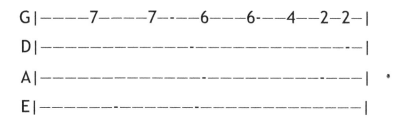

```
G|----7-----7--.--6---6---4--2-2-|
D|----------------.------------.-|
A|------------------.--------.---|
E|-----.------.------------------|
```

```
G|---------.----.--------.-------|
D|-------5-------4---------.----.-|
A|-----------------------.---.---|
E|------.------------------------|
```

```
G|--7----7--6---.--4----2---2---|
D|------------------------------.-|
A|--------------------------.---|
E|------.-----------------------|
```

```
G|————————————.——.———————————————|
D|————————5————4————————4——————|
A|——————————————————————————————.———|
E|—————————.——————————————————————|
```

```
G|—————————————.——.————————.—————————|
D|———4————4——4———4————————————.——|
A|———————————————————————————————.———|
E|—————————.——————————————————————|
```

```
G|—————————.——.————————.——————————|
D|————4————5————7——————————————.—|
A|——————————————————————————.———|
E|—————————.——————————————————————|
```

```
G|-----------------------------------------------|
D|-----5-------4---------2----2----2-|
A|-----------------------------------------------|
E|-----------------------------------------------|


G|-----------------------------------------------|
D|-----2-------4-----5----------------------|
A|-----------------------------------------------|
E|-----------------------------------------------|


G|-----------------------------------------------|
D|-----4-------2-----------0------------|
A|-----------------------------------------------|
E|-----------------------------------------------|
```

```
G|----------7------------------|
D|---------------------------.-|
A|-------------------------.---|
E|-------.---------------------|
```

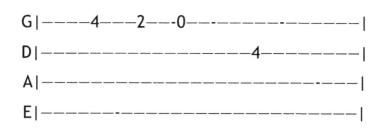

```
G|----4---2--0---.---------.----|
D|--------------------4--------|
A|------------------------.---|
E|-------.-------------------|
```

```
G|----6-----.---.------.------.-|
D|----------4---2----0------.-|
A|-----------------------.---|
E|-------.--------------------|
```

We Wish You a Merry Christmas

```
G|------------------------------------|
D|-------5---5----7--5-------------|
A|--5---------------------------------|
E|------------------------------------|


G|------------------------------------|
D|---4-------------------------------|
A|--------7------7----------------|
E|------------------------------------|


G|------------------------------------|
D|----------7----7----9----7--|
A|----7------------------------------|
E|------------------------------------|
```

```
G|----------------------------------------------|
D|----------------------------------------------|
A|----10-------9-----5----------------|
E|----------------------------------------------|
```

```
G|------------4---4------5-----4----|
D|------------------------------------------7--|
A|----5-------------------------------------|
E|----------------------------------------------|
```

```
G|----------------------------------------------|
D|----5---------------------------------------|
A|--------------7-----5--5----------|
E|----------------------------------------------|
```

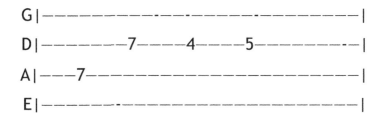

```
G|--------------------.---.-----------------------|
D|-------7----4-----5----------------.--|
A|---7----------------------------------------|
E|-----------------.----------------------|
```

```
G|--------------------.---.---------.----------------|
D|-------5-----5----5-----------4-----4-|
A|---5-------------------------------------------|
E|-----------------.-------------------------------|
```

```
G|---------------------.---.-------.--------------|
D|-----5-----4-----2----0---------.--|
A|-------------------------------------.---|
E|---------------.-----------------------------|
```

```
G|--------4--4---5----4--.-------|
D|---------------------------7---.-|
A|---5------------------------.---|
E|---------------.---------------.--|


G|-----------------.---.--------.---------|
D|-----5----------------------------.--|
A|----------------7-----5----5------.--|
E|-----------.-------------------------.--|


G|------------------.---.----------.---------|
D|--------7--------------4---5------.--|
A|----7------------------------------7---|
E|-----------.-----------------------------|
```

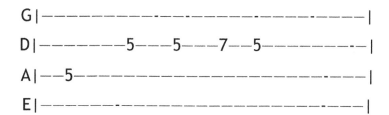

```
G |————————————·——·————————·——·————————|
D |—————————5——5———7——5——————————·—|
A |——5————————————————————————·———|
E |————————·——————————————————·———|
```

```
G |———————————————·——·—————————·——————|
D |———4———————————————————————·—|
A |———————————7—————7——————·————|
E |——————·—————————————————·—————|
```

```
G |———————————————·————·—————————|
D |——————————7————7————9————7——|
A |————7—————————————————————·———|
E |————————·——————————·————————|
```

```
G|----------------------------------------------------|
D|----------------------------------------------------|
A|----10-------9-----5----------------|
E|----------------------------------------------------|
```

```
G|----------4---4------5--------4------|
D|--------------------------------------------7--|
A|----5------------------------------------------|
E|----------------------------------------------------|
```

```
G|----------------------------------------------------|
D|-----5--------------------------------------------|
A|--------------7------5---5-------------|
E|----------------------------------------------------|
```

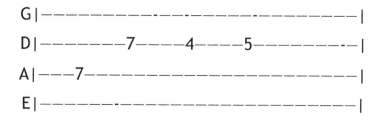

```
G|-------------------------------------------------|
D|-------7-----4-----5------------------.-|
A|----7-----------------------------------------|
E|----------------.----------------------------|
```

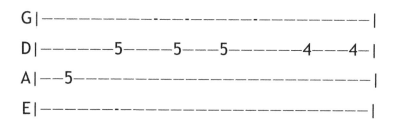

```
G|---------------------.---.-----------.----------|
D|-------5-----5-----5-----------4-----4-|
A|---5-------------------------------------------|
E|------------------.----------------------------|
```

```
G|--------------------.----.----------.----------|
D|-----5-----4-----2----0----------.-|
A|-----------------------------------------.---|
E|-----------.-----------------------------------|
```

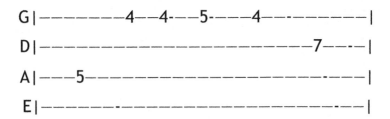

```
G|————————4——4———5————4——-————————|
D|————————————————————————————7———-—|
A|———5——————————————————————————-———|
E|—————————-—————————————————————-—|
```

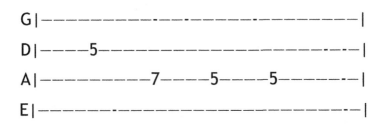

```
G|————————————————-——-————————-————————|
D|————5———————————————————————————-—-—|
A|—————————————7————5————5———————-—|
E|—————————-——————————————————————-—|
```

```
G|——————————————-——-———————-————————|
D|————————7————————4———5———————-—|
A|———7————————————————————————————|
E|—————————-——————————————————————|
```

O Come, O Come Emmanuel

```
G|------------------------------------------|
D|------4-----8-----8----------.-|
A|--6---------------------------------------|
E|-----------.------------------------------|
```

```
G|------------------------------------------|
D|--8--6--9---8---6-----4-----.-|
A|--------------------------------------.----|
E|---------.--------------------------------|
```

```
G|------------------------------------------|
D|--6---8-----4------------------.-|
A|--------------------6---------------------|
E|---------.--------------------------------|
```

```
G|————————————————————————|
D|———4————6——————3——————————--|
A|—————————————————————6——4--—6-|
E|————————————————————————————|
```

```
G|———————————————————————————|
D|——6——6———————————————————--|
A|——————————6—6———8————9————8--|
E|————————————————————————————|
```

```
G|————————————————————————|
D|——————————————————————————--|
A|————6—————4——————————--——|
E|————————————————————————————|
```

```
G|————————————-—————-———————|
D|——4————6—————8——8——8———6—|
A|—————————————————————————-———|
E|————————-————————————————————|
```

```
G|——————————————-———-————-————————|
D|———9——8———6—————4————————————-——|
A|——————————————————————————————-———|
E|————————————-—-——————————————————|
```

```
G|——6———6——————————-———-————————-—|
D|———————————————8———8————————————|
A|————————————————————————————-———|
E|——————————-—————————————————————|
```

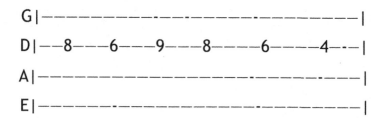

```
G|----------------------------------------|
D|--8---6---9---8----6----4--|
A|----------------------------------------|
E|----------------------------------------|
```

```
G|----------------------------------------|
D|---6--8-----4-------6------|
A|----------------------------------------|
E|----------------------------------------|
```

```
G|----------------------------------------|
D|---4------6----3-------------|
A|------------------------6--4--6--|
E|----------------------------------------|
```

```
G|——————————————————————————————————————|
D|————4————8————8——————————————--|
A|——6—————————————————————————————————————|
E|———————————-————————————————————————————|
```

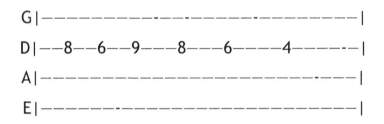

```
G|——————————————————————————————————————|
D|——8——6——9————8————6——————4——————--|
A|————————————————————————————————————-————|
E|———————————-————————————————————————————|
```

```
G|——————————————————————————————————————|
D|——6————8——————4——————————————————--|
A|————————————————————6————————————————|
E|——————————-——————————————————————————|
```

```
G|————————————-—-—————————-—————————|
D|———4————6—————3—————————————————-—|
A|———————————————————————6——4——-—6—|
E|———————————-————————————————————-————|

G|—————————————————-—-——————————-——|
D|——6——6—————————————————————————-—|
A|——————————6—6———8————9————8--—|
E|———————————-———————————————————-————|

G|————————————————-—-————————-————————|
D|—————————————————————————————-—|
A|————6————————4————————————-—-———|
E|———————————-———————————————————————|
```

```
G|---------------------------------------------|
D|---4-----6----------8---8---8----6-|
A|---------------------------------------------|
E|---------------------------------------------|
```

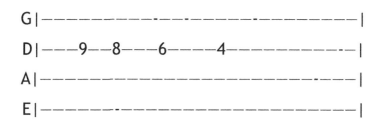

```
G|---------------------------------------------|
D|----9---8----6------4----------------|
A|---------------------------------------------|
E|---------------------------------------------|
```

```
G|--6----6---------------------------------|
D|----------------------8---8------------|
A|---------------------------------------------|
E|---------------------------------------------|
```

```
G|————————————————————·——·——————————·——————————|
D|——8———6———9———8————6————4——·—|
A|————————————————————————·————·—·———|
E|—————————————·———————————·—————————|
```

```
G|——————————————————·——·—————————·—————————|
D|———6——8————4————————6—————·—|
A|————————————————————————————·——|
E|—————————·—————————————·——————————|
```

```
G|————————————————·——·——————·——————————|
D|———4—————6————3————————————·—|
A|———————————————————6——4——-6——|
E|—————————·——————————————————|
```

Hark The Herald Angels Sing

```
G|------------------------------------------------|
D|--------3----3----2----3------------------|
A|----3-------------------------------------|
E|------------------------------------------------|


G|------------------------------------------------|
D|-----7----7----5---------------------------|
A|------------------------------------------------|
E|------------------------------------------------|


G|-------5----5-----5-----------------------|
D|------------------------------------------------|
A|------------------------------------------------|
E|------------------------------------------------|
```

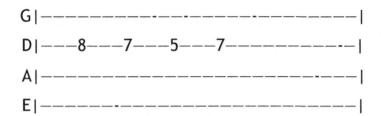

```
G|------------------.--------------.---------------|
D|---8----7----5----7------------------.--|
A|----------------------------------.---|
E|----------.--------------------------------|
```

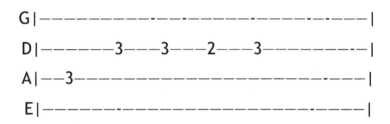

```
G|--------------.---.-------------.----.----|
D|------3----3----2----3-----------.--|
A|--3------------------------------.---|
E|-----------.-----------------------.---|
```

```
G|------------.---.-------------.-------------|
D|-----7----7------------5-------.--|
A|-----------------------------.----|
E|--------.-----------------------------|
```

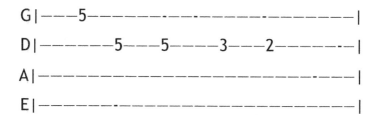

```
G|----5---------------------------------|
D|-------5---5-----3---2---------------|
A|----------------------------------|
E|----------------------------------|
```

```
G|-----------------------------------|
D|-------0---------------------------|
A|-------------3---------------------|
E|-----------------------------------|
```

```
G|-----5---5------5----------------|
D|-----------------------3-------|
A|-----------------------------------|
E|-----------------------------------|
```

```
G|————————————-——-——————-—————————|
D|———8————7———7———5———————————-—|
A|————————————————————————————-———|
E|———————-————————————————————————|
```

```
G|————5——5——5——-————-—3———-————————|
D|———————————————————————————————-—|
A|————————————————————————————-———|
E|——————————-——————————————————————|
```

```
G|————————————————-——-——————-————————|
D|————8————7————7———5————————-—|
A|————————————————————————————-———|
E|—————————-————————————————————————|
```

```
G|----7--7-7----5---3---2---3--.---|
D|--------------------------------.-|
A|-------------------------------.---|
E|--------.-------------------------|
```

```
G|------2---3.--5----------------|
D|---5---------------------------.-|
A|----------------------------.---.---|
E|-----------.---------------.-------|
```

```
G|----------.---0-----------.---------.---|
D|--3---3-----------------------3------.-|
A|----------------------------------.---|
E|----------.---------------------------|
```

```
G|——————————————————·————·——·—————————·————————————|
D|————————3————3————2————3——————————·—|
A|———3———————————————————————————————·————|
E|——————————————·———————————————————·——————|


G|————————————————————·——————·—————————·——————————|
D|—————7————7————5————————————————·—|
A|———————————————————————————————·———|
E|———————————————·————————————————————————|


G|————————5————5·————·5——————·——————————|
D|————————————————————————————————·—|
A|————————————————————————————·———|
E|————————————·————————————————————————|
```

46

```
G|————————————————·———·————————·————————|
D|———8———7———5———7——————————————·—|
A|——————————————————————————————·———|
E|————————·——————————————————————|
```

```
G|——————————————·——·——————————·—·———|
D|——————3———3———2———3————————·—|
A|——3——————————————————————·———|
E|——————————·——————————————·———|
```

```
G|————————————·——·——————————·—————————|
D|————·——7———7———————————5————————·—|
A|——————————————————————————·———|
E|—————————·——————————————————|
```

```
G|———5———————————·——·——————————·——————————|
D|————————5———5————————3———2—————————·——|
A|——————————————————————————————————————————·——|
E|——————————·————————————————————————————————|
```

```
G|——————————————————·——·————————————————————————|
D|——————————0————————————————————————————·—|
A|——————————————————3————————————————————————·———|
E|——————————————·——————————————————————·————————|
```

```
G|—————5———5—·———·—5—————————·——·——|
D|————————————————————————————3————·—|
A|——————————————————————————————————·——|
E|——————————·——————————————————————————|
```

```
G|————————————-—-————————-—————————|
D|———8————7——7——5——————————-—|
A|——————————————————————————————-———|
E|——————————-———————————————————————|
```

```
G|————5——5——5—-————-3———-————————|
A|——————————————————————————————————|
A|——————————————————————————————-———|
E|————————-—————————————————————————|
```

```
G|———————————————-—-—————————-———————|
D|————8————7————7——5————————-—|
A|————————————————————————————-————|
E|————————-————————————————————————|
```

```
G|———7——7—7———5·——3·——2——3——·——|
D|————————————————————————·—|
A|—————————————————————————·———|
E|——————————·——————————————————|
```

```
G|———————2———3·——5·——————————————|
D|———5————————————————————————·—|
A|————————————————————————·———·———|
E|——————————·——————————————·————·———|
```

```
G|———————————·———0·————————·———————·——|
D|——3———3———————————————3——————·—|
A|—————————————————————————·———|
E|————————·——————————————————————|
```

50

12 Days Of Christmas

1st Day

```
G|--------------------4--4--4---3----|
D|--4---4---4-------------------------|
A|-----------------------------------|
E|-----------------------------------|


G|--4---6---8--9--6---8----|
D|-------------------------|
A|-------------------------|
E|-------------------------|


G|---8---9---11---13--9---8---|
D|---------------------------|
A|---------------------------|
E|---------------------------|
```

```
G|------4------6--------4--------|
D|-------------------------------|
A|-------------------------------|
E|-------------------------------|
```

2nd Day

```
G|----------------4----4--4----3--|
D|--4--4---4-----------------------|
A|--------------------------------|
E|--------------------------------|
```

```
G|---4--6---8--9----6----8----|
D|----------------------------|
A|----------------------------|
E|----------------------------|
```

```
G|--11---6---8--·--9---6---------|
D|-------------------------------·--|
A|---------------------------------·---|
E|---------·-----------------------|
```

```
G|--8--9---11--13---9-·---8-----|
D|---------------------------------·--|
A|-----------------------------·---|
E|---------·-----------------------|
```

```
G|----·--4---6--·---·-4----·---·--·--|
D|---------------------------------·--|
A|----------------------------·---|
E|---------·-----------------------|
```

3rd Day

```
G|----------------------4----4--4----3--|
D|--4--4---4--------------------------|
A|-----------------------------------|
E|-----------------------------------|


G|---4--6---8--9--.--6----8----|
D|-----------------------------------|
A|-----------------------------------|
E|-----------------------------------|


G|---11---9----8----.--6----4---|
D|-----------------------------------|
A|-----------------------------------|
E|-----------------------------------|
```

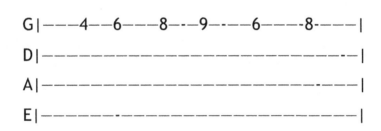

```
G|---9------------- - ---------- -------------|
D|--------------------------------9--------- -|
A|---------------------9----------------- - --|
E|----------- - -------------------------- - -|



G|------------------ - ----------- -----------|
D|---11---9---8-----6---4--- - -- |
A|------------------------------------- - ---|
E|----------- - -----------------------------|



G|---8---9----- -11--13- --9---8- -- |
D|--------------------------------------- - -|
A|-------------------------------- - --------|
E|----------- - -----------------------------|
```

```
G|———————4————·—6—·————4———·————————|
D|————————————————————————————————·—|
A|—————————————————————————————·————|
E|————————·—————————————————————————|
```

4th Day

```
G|————————————·———4————4——4————3——|
D|——4——4———4————————————————————·—|
A|——————————————————————————————·——|
E|————————·————————————————————————|
```

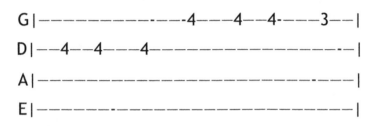

```
G|———4——6———8··—9—·——6————8·————|
D|——————————————————————————————·—|
A|——————————————————————————·———|
E|———————·————————————————————————|
```

```
G|--11----9--8--·--6---4--------|
D|------------------------------·-|
A|--------------------------·---|
E|---------·--------------------|
```

```
G|---9-----------·---------·-----|
D|-----------------------9-----·--|
A|---------------9----------·---|
E|--------·----------------·----|
```

```
G|-----------·--·------·------|
D|---11---9--8----6---4--·--·-|
A|------------------------·---|
E|------·--------------------|
```

```
G|---8---9----11--13---9---8--|
D|---------------------------.-|
A|--------------------------.---|
E|-------.---------------------|


G|------4---.-6--.--4--.------|
D|---------------------------.-|
A|--------------------------.---|
E|-------.---------------------|
```

5th Day

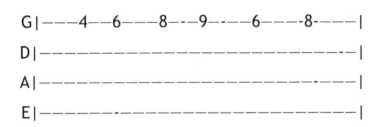

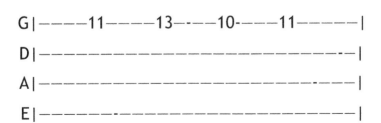

```
G|--11----9--8--.--6---4---------|
D|------------------------------.-|
A|--------------------------.----|
E|---------.----------------------|
```

```
G|---9--------------.---.-----------.---------|
D|----------------------------9-----------.--|
A|--------------9---------------------.---|
E|---------.--------------.----------.----|
```

```
G|------------------.----.----------.----------|
D|---11---9---8----6---4---.--.--|
A|-----------------------------------.----|
E|---------.----------.-----------------|
```

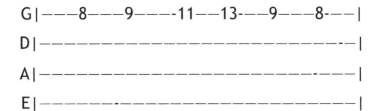

```
G|---8---9----11--13---9---8---|
D|----------------------------------|
A|----------------------------------|
E|---------------------------------|
```

```
G|------4----6----4--------|
D|----------------------------------|
A|----------------------------------|
E|---------------------------------|
```

6th Day

```
G|----------------4---4--4----3--|
D|--4--4---4---------------------|
A|------------------------------|
E|------------------------------|
```

```
G|---4--6---8--9----6----8----|
D|-----------------------------|
A|-----------------------------|
E|-----------------------------|
```

```
G|----11---6----8----9---6------|
D|------------------------------|
A|------------------------------|
E|------------------------------|
```

```
G|————11————13——-——10————11————|
D|——————————————————————————--|
A|———————————————————————-————|
E|———————-——————————————————|
```

```
G|——11————9——8——-——6———4————————|
D|——————————————————————————--|
A|————————————————————————-———|
E|————————-——————————————————|
```

```
G|———9—————————-——-—————————————|
D|——————————————————9————————--|
A|————————————9——————————————-———|
E|—————————-——————————————--——|
```

```
G|————————————————————————————————————|
D|———11———9———8————6———4——————————————|
A|————————————————————————————————————|
E|————————————————————————————————————|
```

```
G|———8———9————-11——13-———9———8————|
A|————————————————————————————————|
A|————————————————————————————————|
E|————————————————————————————————|
```

```
G|—————————4————-6——-———4——————————|
D|—————————————————————————————————|
A|—————————————————————————————————|
E|—————————————————————————————————|
```

7th Day

```
G|--11--11---6---·-8---9---6---|
D|-------------------------------|
A|-------------------------------|
E|----------·-------------------·---|
```

```
G|----11----6---.-8--.--9----6-----.|
D|-------------------------------.-|
A|-------------------------.---|
E|---------.-------------------------|
```

```
G|-----11-----13--.--10-----11------|
D|----------------------------.-|
A|------------------------.----|
E|-----------.-------------------|
```

```
G|--11-----9--8--.---6---4------|
D|---------------------------.-|
A|-----------------------.---|
E|----------.---------------------|
```

```
G|---9-----------.---.----------.--------|
D|-----------------------------9-------.-|
A|--------------------9---------------.---|
E|---------.----------------------.---.--|
```

```
G|----------------.---.--------.---------|
D|---11---9---8-----6---4---.--.-|
A|------------------------------------.---|
E|----------.---------------------------|
```

```
G|---8---9----.-11--13-.--9---8-.--|
D|------------------------------------.-|
A|-------------------------------.---|
E|----------.-------------------------|
```

```
G|-------4------6-----4---------|
D|----------------------------|
A|----------------------------|
E|----------------------------|
```

8th Day

```
G|---------------4---4--4-----3--|
D|--4--4---4---------------------|
A|-------------------------------|
E|-------------------------------|
```

```
G|---4--6---8--9----6----8----|
D|---------------------------|
A|---------------------------|
E|---------------------------|
```

```
G|--11----6---8----9----6--·----|
D|--------------------------·-|
A|---------------------·---|
E|-------·--------------|
```

```
G|--11--11---6--·-8---9--6---|
D|-------------------------|
A|-------------------------|
E|------·------------·---|
```

```
G|----11---6--·-8--·-9--6----·|
D|------------------------·-|
A|----------------------·--|
E|------·-----------------|
```

```
G|-----11-----13--·--10-----11-----|
D|-------------------------------·--|
A|----------------------------·---|
E|---------·----------------------|
```

```
G|--11-----9--8--·--6·---4-------|
D|--------------------------·--|
A|----------------------------·---|
E|---------·----------------------|
```

```
G|---9--------------·----------·--------|
D|----------------------9-------·--|
A|---------------9-------------·---|
E|---------·-------------------·----|
```

```
G|——————————————————————————|
D|———11———9———8————6———4——-——|
A|——————————————————————————|
E|——————-————————————————————|
```

```
G|———8———9————11——13———9———8———|
D|——————————————————————————-——|
A|——————————————————————————-——|
E|——————————-—————————————————|
```

```
G|————————4—————-—6—-———4——-————————|
D|————————————————————————————-——|
A|————————————————————————-———|
E|————————-————————————————————|
```

9th Day

```
G|————————-——-4———4——4-———3——|
D|——4——4———4————————————————-—|
A|————————————————————————-——|
E|————————-———————————————————|
```

```
G|———4——6———8--—9-·———6———-8-———|
D|——————————————————————————-·—|
A|—————————————————————————-———|
E|————————-———————————————————|
```

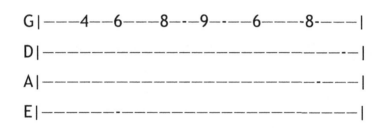

```
G|———11——————6--·——-8——9————6--·——|
D|—————————————————————————————-·—|
A|—————————————————————————-·———|
E|—————————-——————————————————|
```

```
G|--11-----6---8----9-----6--------|
D|-------------------------------|
A|-------------------------------|
E|-------------------------------|
```

```
G|--11--11----6----8---9---6----|
D|-------------------------------|
A|-------------------------------|
E|-------------------------------|
```

```
G|-----11---6----8-----9---6------|
D|-------------------------------|
A|-------------------------------|
E|-------------------------------|
```

```
G|----11-----13--.--10----11------|
D|-------------------------------.--|
A|-------------------------------.---|
E|------------.--------------------|
```

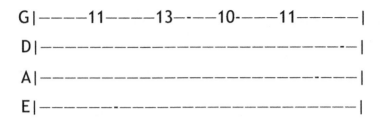

```
G|--11-----9--8--.--6---4--------|
D|-------------------------------.-|
A|-----------------------------.---|
E|----------.---------------------|
```

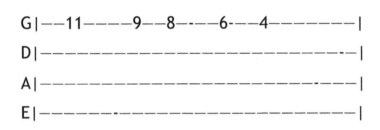

```
G|---9----------.---.-----------.---------|
D|-------------------------9-------.-|
A|----------9--------------------.---|
E|----------.------------------.---|
```

```
G|————————————————————————————————|
D|———11———9———8————6———4——————|
A|————————————————————————————————|
E|————————————————————————————————|
```

```
G|———8———9————11—13———9———8———|
A|————————————————————————————————|
D|————————————————————————————————|
E|————————————————————————————————|
```

```
G|————————4————6——————4————————————|
D|————————————————————————————————|
A|————————————————————————————————|
E|————————————————————————————————|
```

10th Day

```
G|--------------------4---4--4----3--|
D|--4--4---4-------------------------|
A|----------------------------------|
E|------------------------------------|
```

```
G|---4--6---8--9---6----8----|
D|---------------------------|
A|---------------------------|
E|---------------------------|
```

```
G|---11-----6---8--9-----6----|
D|----------------------------|
A|----------------------------|
E|----------------------------|
```

```
G|———11—————6——————8——9————6——-——|
D|——————————————————————————————-—|
A|———————————————————————————-———|
E|——————————-——————————————————|
```

```
G|——11—————6———8————9————6——-—————|
D|—————————————————————————————-—|
A|————————————————————————————-———|
E|—————————-————————————————————|
```

```
G|——11——11———6———-—8———9———6———|
D|———————————————————————————————|
A|—————————————————————————————|
E|———————-—————————————————-———|
```

```
G|----11---6---·8--·--9---6----·|
D|-----------------------------·-|
A|-----------------------·--·--|
E|-------·---------------------|
```

```
G|----11-----13--·--10----11-----|
D|-----------------------------·-|
A|--------------------------·--·--|
E|--------·---------------------|
```

```
G|--11-----9--8--·--6--·4------|
D|--------------------------·-·|
A|------------------------·-·--|
E|------·----------------------|
```

```
G|———9—————————  —  —  —————  —————|
D|————————————————————9————————-—|
A|————————————9——————————————————|
E|————————————————————————————————|
```

```
G|————————————  —  ————————  ————————|
D|———11———9———8————6———4——-—-—|
A|————————————————————————————————|
E|————————-—————————————————————|
```

```
G|——8———9————-11—13-——9———8-——|
D|——————————————————————————————-—|
A|————————————————————————————————|
E|————————-——————————————————————|
```

```
G|———————4————·—6——·————4——·—·————————|
D|—————————————————————————————————————·—|
A|———————————————————————————————————·————|
E|—————————·—————————————————————————————|
```

11th Day

```
G|———————————————·———4———4——4—·———3——|
D|——4——4———4——————————————————————·—|
A|————————————————————————————————————·———|
E|————————·————————————————————————————|
```

```
G|———4——6———8—·—9—·—·———6————·8·————|
D|—————————————————————————————————————·—|
A|———————————————————————————————————·————|
E|———————·—————————————————————————————|
```

```
G|--11--11----11----6---8--9--8--|
D|------------------------------ --|
A|------------------------------- ---|
E|----------- -------------------------|


G|---11----6---.-8---.9-----6----|
D|------------------------------ --|
A|------------------------------- ---|
E|----------- -------------------------|


G|---11-----6--.---8--9----6--.--|
D|------------------------------ --|
A|------------------------------- ---|
E|------- --------------------------|
```

```
G|---11-----6---8----9-----6--·-----|
D|------------------------------·-·—|
A|----------------------------·---—|
E|----------·-----------------------|
```

```
G|---11---11----6---·-8----9---6---|
D|--------------------------------—|
A|--------------------------------—|
E|---------------·----------------·-·--|
```

```
G|-----11---6---·-8--·--9---6-----·|
D|------------------------------·--—|
A|--------------------------·-·--—|
E|-------·---------------------—|
```

```
G|----11----13--·--10----11-----|
D|-------------------------·-|
A|------------------------·---|
E|-------·-------------------|
```

```
G|--11----9--8--·--6---4------|
D|--------------------------·-|
A|------------------------·---|
E|-------·-------------------|
```

```
G|---9----------------·--------·-----------|
D|--------------------------9------·-|
A|---------------9-----------·---|
E|------·-------------------·-·--|
```

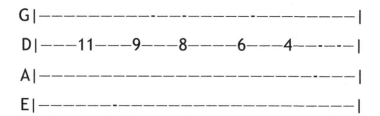

```
G|----------------------------------|
D|---11---9---8-----6---4----------|
A|----------------------------------|
E|----------------------------------|
```

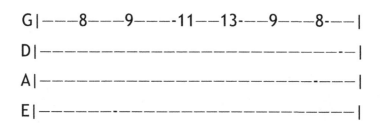

```
G|---8---9----11--13---9---8---|
D|----------------------------------|
A|----------------------------------|
E|----------------------------------|
```

```
G|--------4-----6-----4------------|
D|----------------------------------|
A|----------------------------------|
E|----------------------------------|
```

12th Day

```
G|----------------------4----4---4-----3---|
D|---4---4-----4------------------------------|
A|----------------------------------------------|
E|--------------------------------------------|
```

```
G|----4---6-----8---9------6------8------|
D|---------------------------------------------|
A|---------------------------------------------|
E|---------------------------------------------|
```

```
G|----11-----6----8------9-----6---|
D|--------------------------------------------|
A|--------------------------------------------|
E|--------------------------------------------|
```

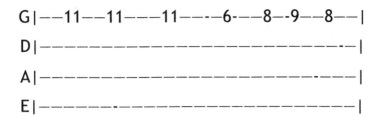

```
G|--11--11----11---·-6---8--9--8--|
D|-----------------------------·-|
A|-----------------------------·--|
E|-----------·-------------------|
```

```
G|---11----6---·-8--·9-----6----|
D|-----------------------------·-|
A|-----------------------------·--|
E|---------·--------------------|
```

```
G|---11-----6--·--8--9----6--·--|
D|-----------------------------·-|
A|----------------------------·--|
E|--------·---------------------|
```

```
G|--11----6---8----9----6--.----|
D|-----------------------------.-|
A|----------------------------.---|
E|------------.------------------|
```

```
G|--11--11---6---.-8---9---6----|
D|-------------------------------|
A|-------------------------------|
E|--------.---.----------------.--|
```

```
G|----11---6--.-8-.--9---6----.|
D|------------------------------.-|
A|--------------------------.---|
E|--------.-----------------------|
```

```
G|-----11-----13---·--10-----11-----|
D|--------------------------------·-|
A|-------------------------------·---|
E|---------·-------------------------|
```

```
G|--11-----9--8--·--6---4--------|
D|--------------------------------·-|
A|------------------------------·---|
E|------------·---------------------|
```

```
G|---9--------------·---·----------·---------|
D|--------------------------9-------·-|
A|--------------9-----------------·---|
E|----------·--------------------·---|
```

```
G|————————————————————————|
D|———11———9———8————6———4——————|
A|————————————————————————|
E|————————————————————————|
```

```
G|———8———9————11——13———9———8———|
A|————————————————————————|
D|————————————————————————|
E|————————————————————————|
```

```
G|——————4————6————4——————————|
D|————————————————————————|
A|————————————————————————|
E|————————————————————————|
```

Once In Royal David's City

```
G|————————7————-—8——-—8————8——-—7———8——|
D|——8———————————————————————————————————|
A|——————————————————————————————————-———|
E|————————————-—————————————————————————|


G|———10—————10——-———-—8————————-————-——|
D|————————————————————————————————————-—|
A|————————————————————————————————-————|
E|——————————————-———————————————————————|


G|————8—————12——-———-———15—————————————|
D|————————————————————————————————————-—|
A|——————————————————————————————————-———|
E|——————————————-———————————————————————|
```

```
G|----12-------12----.------10------|
D|----------------------------------.--|
A|-------------------------------.----|
E|-----------.---------------------|
```

```
G|-------8---.----7------.8------|
D|---------------------------------.--|
A|-------------------------------.----|
E|-----------.---------------------|
```

```
G|-------7----.8---8---8--.-7--8--|
D|--8---------------------------------|
A|--------------------------------.---|
E|----------.---------------------|
```

```
G|———10————10——-——-—8———————-————|
D|————————————————————————————————-—|
A|—————————————————————————————-———|
E|——————————-———————————————————————|
```

```
G|————8————12——-———-——15————————|
D|—————————————————————————————————-—|
A|————————————————————————————————-————|
E|——————————-——————————————————————|
```

```
G|————12——————12-——-————10—————|
D|————————————————————————————————-—|
A|————————————-————————————————-———|
E|——————————-————————————————————|
```

```
G|-------8---.---7------8-----|
D|----------------------------.-|
A|------------------------.---|
E|--------.-------------------|
```

```
G|-------5--.5--.-----3------|
D|---------------------------.-|
A|-----------------------.---|
E|-------.-------------------|
```

```
G|----------1-.--.-1----.-0---.-|
D|----1----------------------.-|
A|----------------------.-.---|
E|-------.-------------------|
```

```
G|———5———5————-3—-——0————-—0———-—|
D|——————————————————————————————-—|
A|——————————————————————————————-———|
E|————————-—————————————————————————|
```

```
G|———————————————-———————————-————————|
D|———3————1—————0—————————1——-—|
A|——————————————————————————————-———|
E|————————-————————————————————————|
```

```
G|————————7———-—8—-—8———8—-—7——8——|
D|——8————————————————————————————|
A|—————————————————————————————-———|
E|————————-—————————————————————————|
```

```
G|———10—————10———·——·—8———————·——·——|
D|————————————————————————————————·—|
A|————————————————————————————·——·—|
E|————————·———————————————————————|
```


```
G|————8—————12——·——·———15—————————|
D|————————————————————————————————·—|
A|————————————————————————————·—·——|
E|————————·————————————————————————|
```


```
G|————12————————12———·——·————10—————|
D|————————————————————————————————·—|
A|——————————————————————————————·—·——|
E|————————·————————————————————————|
```

```
G |————————8————·———7————·—8—————|
D |————————————————————————————·—|
A |————————————————————————————·————|
E |—————————·——————————————————————|
```

```
G |—————7———·—8——·8———8——·—7——8——|
D |——8————————————————————————————|
A |————————————————————————————·———|
E |—————————·——————————————————————|
```

```
G |———10—————10———·———·—8————————·———·———|
D |————————————————————————————————·—|
A |—————————————————————————————·———|
E |——————————·—————————————————————————|
```

```
G|————8————12——-———15—————————|
D|—————————————————————————————-—|
A|———————————————————————————-———|
E|———————-——————————————————————|
```

```
G|————12—————12————-——————10—————|
D|——————————————————————————————-—|
A|————————————————————————————-———|
E|——————————-———————————————————|
```

```
G|——————8——-————7——————--8—————|
D|——————————————————————————————-—|
A|—————————————————————————-———|
E|————————-————————————————————|
```

```
G|————————5——-5——-——————3—————|
D|————————————————————————————————————-—|
A|—————————————————————————————————————-———|
E|————————-——————————————————————————————|
```

```
G|——————————————1-——-—1————-——0——-—|
D|————1——————————————————————————-—|
A|——————————————————————————————————-———|
E|——————————-————————————————————|
```

```
G|———5———5————-—3——-——0——————0——-—|
D|————————————————————————————————————-—|
A|——————————————————————————————-———|
E|————————-————————————————————|
```

```
G|————————————.——-—————————.————————|
D|———3————1————0————————1——-—|
A|——————————————————————————————-———|
E|———————————.-——————————————————————|
```

Away in a Manger

```
G|----5---5-----7---9--.--5---5-|
D|-5----------.---------------.--|
A|-----------------------------.---|
E|----------.----------------------|
```

```
G|---9----10---.---12----12--.---|
D|---------------------------------.--|
A|-----------------------------.---|
E|----------.----------------------|
```

```
G|--14-------.-10---.----------.----|
D|---------------------------------.--|
A|-----------------------------.---|
E|----------.----------------------|
```

```
G|----7--9--10---·---12----9-----9--|
D|----------------------------------·--|
A|--------------------------------·---|
E|--------·-------------------------|
```

```
G|------5-----9-----·--7---------·--------|
D|---------------------------------------·--|
A|------------------------------------·----|
E|------------·---------------------------|
```

```
G|-----------------·---·-------·----------|
D|----7-----10-------·--9----------·--|
A|---------------------------------·---|
E|--------·-----------------------------|
```

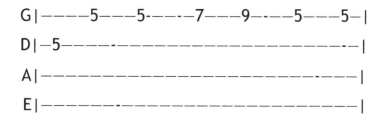

```
G|----5---5---.--7---9--.--5---5-|
D|-5----------.--------------.-|
A|------------------------.---|
E|----------.---------------|
```

```
G|---9----10---.---12-----12-.--|
D|---------------------------.-|
A|------------------------.---|
E|----------.---------------|
```

```
G|--14-------10--.-------.----|
D|---------------------------.-|
A|------------------------.---|
E|----------.---------------|
```

```
G|---7--9--10---.---12.---9-----9--|
D|------------------------------.--|
A|-----------------------------.---|
E|--------.------------------------|
```

```
G|-----5-----9-.---.-7----.--------|
D|-----------------------------.--|
A|--------------------------.---|
E|--------.----------------------|
```

```
G|-----------.--.------.--------|
D|---7----9------10---------.--|
A|--------------------------.---|
E|------.-----------------------|
```

Jingle Bells

```
G|------------------------------------------------------|
D|--------14------12--------10--------------|
A|---10-------------------------------10-----|
E|------------------------------------------------------|


G|------------------------------------------------------|
D|------------------------14----12--------------|
A|-10---10---10-----------------------------------|
E|------------------------------------------------------|


G|------------------------------------------------------|
D|------10-----------------------------------------|
A|-----------------12--------------------------------|
E|------------------------------------------------------|
```

```
G|------10-----.---9-------.----------|
D|-------------------------12---9-----.--|
A|-12-------------------------------|
E|----------.---------------------.--.----|
```

```
G|----12----12-----.10---.------7--.--9-|
D|-------------------------------.--|
A|----------------------------.---|
E|----------.--------------------|
```

```
G|------------.--.------.-------|
D|------14---12-----10----------.--|
A|-10-------------------.--10--.----|
E|-------.--.---------------.------|
```

```
G|——————————————————————————·———·——————————·——————————|
D|——————14———12————————10———————————————————·—|
A|—10———————————————————————————·—12——·————|
E|————————————·—————————————————————————·———————|
```

```
G|————————————————————·———·——————————·—————————————|
D|——————————————————————————————————————————·——|
A|——————————————12————————————————————·————————·———|
E|————————————·—————————————————————————·————————|
```

```
G|——————————10———·—9——·—·——————————·—————————|
D|—————————————————————————————12————————·—|
A|——12——————————————————————————————————·———|
E|————————————·———————————————————————·———|
```

```
G|-----12-----12--·---12----------·----|
D|-------------------------------------·--|
A|----------------------------------·---|
E|----------·--------------------------|
```

```
G|--12----12------·14---·---12------|
D|---------------------------------------·--|
A|--------------------------------·---|
E|--------·--------------------------|
```

```
G|--10------------·---·-----12------|
D|-------12----10-------------·--|
A|---------------------------------·---|
E|--------·------------------------|
```

```
G|———9——9———9—·—/—9———9———9———|
D|———————————————————————————————|
A|———————————————————————————·———|
E|———————————·———————————————————|
```

```
G|——————9———12—·———·———————·———————9——|
D|——————————————————————10————12———————·——|
A|————————————————————————————————·—·——|
E|————————————·———————————————————·———|
```

```
G|—10————10—————·10——·———·——————————|
D|———————————————————————————————·——|
A|—————————————————————————————·———|
E|————————·——————————————————————|
```

```
G|----10----10----.---9-------9--.--|
D|--------------------------------.--|
A|----------------------------.----|
E|--------.------------------------|
```

```
G|----9-----9--.---12----12--10---|
D|------------------------------.--|
A|---------------------------.---|
E|--------.---------------------|
```

```
G|----------------.-12----.------|
D|----12---------10----------.--|
A|-----------------------.---|
E|------.---------------------|
```

```
G|————————————————————————————————|
D|————————14—————12—————————10————————-—|
A|——10——————————————————————————--————10--————|
E|————————————-—————————————————————————————-———————|

G|————————————————————-—————————————————-—————————————|
D|——————————————————————————14————12—————————|
A|—10————10————10————————————————————————————-————|
E|————————————————-—————————————————————————————————|

G|————————————————————————-—————————————————-—————————|
D|—————————10————————————————————————————————————-——|
A|————————————————12————————————————————————-—————|
E|————————————-————————————————————————————-—————————|
```

```
G|------10----.--9--------.-----------|
D|---------------------12---9-----.--|
A|-12-----------------------------------|
E|-----------.--------------------.--.---|
```

```
G|----12----12-----.10--.-------7---.--9-|
D|--------------------------------.--|
A|---------------------------.----|
E|-----------.-------------------------|
```

```
G|------------------.--.-------.----------|
D|------14---12-----.10--------.--|
A|-10-----------------------.-10--.----|
E|--------------.--------------.------|
```

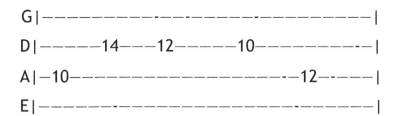

```
G|————————————————————————————————————|
D|————14————12—————————10—————————————--|
A|—10———————————————————————————————12——--————|
E|—————————————————————————————————————————|
```

```
G|————————————————————————————————————|
D|———————————————————————————————————————--|
A|———————————————12—————————————————————--—————|
E|——————————————————————————————————————|
```

```
G|————————————10——--9——--———————————————————--——|
D|—————————————————————————————————12—————————--—|
A|——12—————————————————————————————————————--————|
E|—————————————————————————————————————————--———|
```

```
G|-----12-----12--·----12----------·----|
D|------------------------------------·--|
A|-----------------------------------·---|
E|---------·-----------------------------|
```

```
G|--12----12------·14---·---12------|
D|------------------------------------·--|
A|-----------------------------·---·---|
E|---------·-·-------------------------|
```

```
G|--10-----------·---·--------12------|
D|-------12-----10------------------·--|
A|----------------------------·------|
E|---------·------------------------|
```

```
G|---9--9---9--./-9---9---9---|
D|-------------------------.-|
A|--------------------------.---|
E|----------.-----------------|
```

```
G|-----9---12-.---.-----------.-----9--|
D|----------------10----12------.-|
A|--------------------------------.-.-|
E|----------.------------------.---|
```

```
G|-10----10-----.10--.----------|
D|---------------------------.-|
A|-----------------------------.---|
E|--------.--------------------|
```

```
G|-----10----10----.---9--------9---.---|
D|------------------------------------.--|
A|-------------------------------.----|
E|------------.--------------------------|
```

```
G|-----9----9---.----12----12--10----|
D|---------------------------------.--|
A|------------------------------.----|
E|-----------.-----------------------|
```

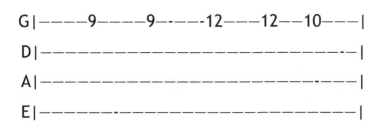

```
G|-------------------.-12-----.-------|
D|-----12---------------10----------.--|
A|-----------------------------.----|
E|---------.-------------------------|
```

Deck the Halls

```
G|--7-----5------4--------------------|
D|---------------------------7----5---|
A|------------------------------------|
E|------------------------------------|


G|---------------4--------------------|
D|--7--------------------------5------|
A|------------------------------------|
E|------------------------------------|


G|-------4----5------------------4-----|
D|--7----------------------7-----------|
A|------------------------------------|
E|------------------------------------|
```

```
G|————————————·—·————————·—————————|
D|———7————5————————4————5————————·—|
A|——————————————————————————————·———|
E|———————————·——————————————————————|
```

```
G|——7————5————·——4—·————·——————·————·—|
D|——————————————————————————7————5———|
A|————————————————————————————————·———|
E|———————————·————————————————————————|
```

```
G|————————4——·——·————·————·————————|
D|——7————————————————————5————————|
A|——————————————————————————·———|
E|———————————·————————————————————|
```

```
G|——————4———5—————————-4————|
D|——7———————————————7———————|
A|——————————————————————————-——|
E|—————————-————————————————|


G|——————————————-——-—————————-——————|
D|———7————5——————4———5———————-—|
A|————————————————————————————-———|
E|————————-—————————————————|


G|—————————4——-——5-——————————-————-——|
D|——7——————————————————7—————|
A|————————————————————————————-———|
E|——————————-————————————————|
```

```
G|---4---5----·---7·-----4-·-------|
D|--------------------------------·-|
A|------------------------------·----|
E|-------·--------------------------|
```

```
G|--7---9---11-·-11-·-12----14·-|
D|--------------------------------·-|
A|------------------------------·----|
E|-------·--------------------------|
```

```
G|--12----11----·--7·-----------|
D|--------------------------------·-|
A|------------------------------·----|
E|-------·--------------------------|
```

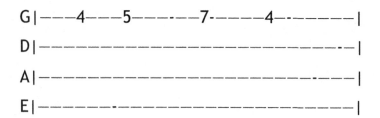

```
G|---2------------------------------------------------|
D|-----------5--4----2--0------2------|
A|------------------------------------------------|
E|------------------------------------------------|
```

```
G|------------------------------------------------|
D|---------4--------0------------------|
A|------------------------------------------------|
E|------------------------------------------------|
```

```
G|------------------------------------------------|
D|--2--4----5---2---4------------------|
A|------------------------------------------------|
E|------------------------------------------------|
```

```
G|————————————·—·—————————·———————————·——|
D|————2————0—————————————————————0—————|
A|———————————————————4———————————————·———|
E|————————————·——————————————————————·——|
```

```
G|——7————5————·——4——·————————·————·—|
D|————————————————————————7————5———|
A|——————————————————————————————————·———|
E|————————————·—————————————————————|
```

```
G|————————4——·——·——————·————————|
D|——7———————————————————5————————|
A|——————————————————————————·———·———|
E|————————————·———————————————————|
```

```
G|--------4----5--------------4------|
D|---7---------------------7----------|
A|-----------------------------------|
E|-------------------------------------|
```

```
G|---------------------------------------|
D|----7-----5--------4-----5----------|
A|-----------------------------------|
E|-------------------------------------|
```

```
G|--7----5-----4-----------------|
D|------------------------7----5----|
A|-----------------------------------|
E|-------------------------------------|
```

```
G|----------4--------------------------|
D|---7--------------------5-------|
A|-------------------------------------|
E|-------------------------------------|
```

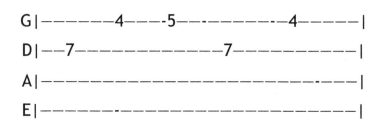

```
G|------4----5------------4-----|
D|--7-----------------7-----------|
A|-------------------------------------|
E|-------------------------------------|
```

```
G|-------------------------------------|
D|---7-----5------4----5-------|
A|-------------------------------------|
E|-------------------------------------|
```

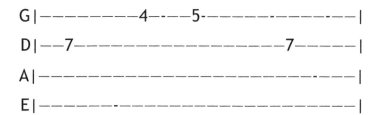

```
G|————————4——5——————————————|
D|——7————————————————————7————|
A|————————————————————————————|
E|————————————————————————————|
```

```
G|————4———5————————7————————4——————|
D|————————————————————————————————|
A|————————————————————————————————|
E|————————————————————————————————|
```

```
G|——7————9————11————11————12————————14——|
D|————————————————————————————————————|
A|————————————————————————————————————|
E|————————————————————————————————————|
```

```
G|--12------11------.--7-----------------|
D|----------------------------------.---|
A|------------------------------------.--|
E|----------------.----------------------|
```

```
G|---2-------------.----.-----------.--------|
D|----------5--4---2--0-----2--.---|
A|---------------------------------------.--|
E|-----------------.--------------------|
```

```
G|-----------------.----.------------.--------|
D|-------4------------0------------.----------.--|
A|---------------------------------------.----|
E|--------------.-----------------------|
```

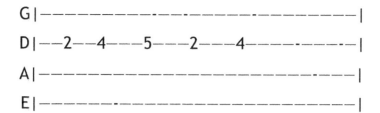

```
G|————————————————————————————————————|
D|——2——4———5———2———4—————————————————|
A|————————————————————————————————————|
E|————————————————————————————————————|
```

```
G|————————————————————————————————————|
D|———2———0———————————————————0—————|
A|——————————————————4———————————————|
E|————————————————————————————————————|
```

O Holy Night

```
G|------------6---6------8--8----|
D|-8--8--8---------------------9-|
A|-----------------------------|
E|-----------------------------|


G|--8--11--6--------------------|
D|----------------8-----8-------|
A|-----------------------------|
E|-----------------------------|


G|-----------------------------|
D|---6----------6------8----|
A|-------9--------------------|
E|-----------------------------|
```

```
G|————6———————·——·——————·————————|
D|——————————8————6———————————————|
A|——————————————————————————9———·——|
E|—————————·——————————————————·————|
```


```
G|——————————6-——6-—————8——8————|
D|-8——8——8——————————————————9-|
A|——————————————————————————·———|
E|—————————·————————————————————|
```


```
G|——8——11——6———————·——·————————·———·——|
D|————————————————8————8—————|
A|——————————————————————————·———|
E|—————————·————————————————————|
```

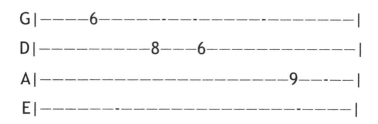

```
G|———11————10————8-———10—————-————|
D|——————————————————————————————-—|
A|———————————————————————————-———|
E|————————-———————————————————————|
```

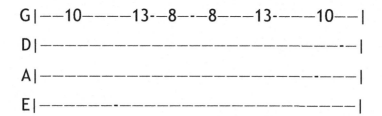

```
G|--10-----13--8--·-8----13-----10--|
D|-----------------------------------·-|
A|-----------------------------·---|
E|-------------·----------------------|
```

```
G|------------·-8-----------·--------|
D|-----------------------------------·-|
A|---------------------------·---|
E|----------·-------------------------|
```

```
G|--11----15---------·----·---11--·--·--|
D|----------------11------------·--·--|
A|--------------------------·----|
E|----------·-------------------------|
```

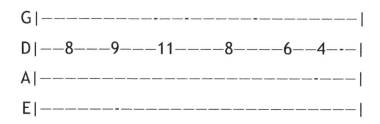

```
G|--8--11--6----------------------------.--|
D|-------------------8------8------|
A|----------------------------------.----|
E|------------.--------------------------|
```

```
G|-------------------.---.-----------.--------|
D|---6-------------6-------8-----.--|
A|----------9-------------------------|
E|-----------.------------------------|
```

```
G|-----6---------.----.----------.--------|
D|----------8---6------------------|
A|------------------------------9---.--|
E|-----------.-----------------.----|
```

```
G|------------6---6-------8--8----|
D|-8--8--8----------------------9-|
A|---------------------------------|
E|---------------------------------|


G|--8--11--6------------------------|
D|------------------8----8----|
A|-----------------------------------|
E|-----------------------------------|


G|------------------------------------|
D|---6------------6------8----|
A|--------9--------------------------|
E|-----------------------------------|
```

```
G|————6———————————.——————.———————————————|
D|——————————8———6————————————————|
A|——————————————————————9————.——|
E|——————————————.—————————————————————.————|

G|———11————10————8————-10—————————.————|
D|——————————————————————————————————————.——|
A|————————————————————————————————.———|
E|—————————————.————————————————————————|

G|——10—————13——8——.——8————13——————10——|
D|————————————————————————————————————.——|
A|—————————————————————————————————.————|
E|—————————————.———————————————————————|
```

```
G|———————————-8———————————————|
D|————————————————————————————-|
A|————————————————————————————-———|
E|——————————-————————————————————|


G|——11———15————————-——-————11———-——-——|
D|————————————————11—————————————-——-|
A|————————————————————————————————-———|
E|—————————-————————————————————————|


G|——————————————————-——-—————————-—————————|
D|——11———————8————————————4———————-——|
A|————————————————————————————————-———|
E|——————————-————————————————————|
```

```
G|————————————--——--———————--—————————|
D|——8———9————11————8————6——4—-——|
A|————————————————————————————-———|
E|—————————-———————————————————————|
```

Merry Christmas and a Happy New Year!

Made in the USA
Coppell, TX
16 November 2022

86485205R00090